Native Americans

The Hopi

Barbara A. Gray-Kanatiiosh

ABDO Publishing Company

visit us at
www.abdopublishing.com

Published by ABDO Publishing Company, 8000 West 78th Street, Edina, Minnesota 55439. Copyright © 2002 by Abdo Consulting Group, Inc. International copyrights reserved in all countries. No part of this book may be reproduced in any form without written permission from the publisher.

Printed in the United States of America, North Mankato, Minnesota.
012002 042012

Illustrations: Charles Chimerica
Interior Photos: Corbis

Editors: Tamara L. Britton, Kate A. Furlong, Kristin Van Cleaf
Art Direction & Maps: Neil Klinepier

Library of Congress Cataloging-in-Publication Data

Gray-Kanatiiosh, Barbara A., 1963-
   The Hopi / Barbara A. Gray-Kanatiiosh
    p. cm. -- (Native Americans)
   Includes index.
   ISBN 1-57765-598-2
   1. Hopi Indians--Juvenile literature. [1. Hopi Indians. 2. Indians of North America--Arizona.] I. Title. II. Native Americans (Edina, Minn.)

E99.H7 G72 2002
979. 1004'9745--dc21

                                                         2001022481

About the Author: Barbara A. Gray-Kanatiiosh, JD

Barbara Gray-Kanatiiosh, JD, is an Akwesasne Mohawk. She has a Juris Doctorate from Arizona State University, where she was one of the first recipients of ASU's special certificate in Indian Law. She is currently pursuing a Ph.D. in Justice Studies at ASU and is focusing on Native American issues. Barbara works hard to educate children about Native Americans through her writing and Web site where children may ask questions and receive a written response about the Haudenosaunee culture. The Web site is: www.peace4turtleisland.org

Illustrator: Charles Chimerica

Charles Chimerica is a Hopi and a member of the Rabbit Clan. An accomplished artist, Charles works with many art forms, including watercolor, pastel, pencil, and acrylic. "I get my ideas by looking at different artists' pieces, thinking, and dreaming," he says. "I always paint with good thoughts and a good heart, and always say a prayer. I never put bad things or thoughts into my pictures. It's like carving a kachina doll; you are drawing yourself into the picture." Charles lives in Glendale, Arizona, but participates in ceremony at Third Mesa.

Contents

Where They Lived 4

Society 6

Food 8

Homes 10

Clothing 12

Crafts 14

Family 16

Children 18

Myths 20

War 22

Contact with Europeans 24

Yokiuma 26

The Hopi Today 28

Glossary 31

Web Sites 31

Index 32

Where They Lived

The name Hopi comes from the word *Hopituh* or *Hopiikwa*, which means Peaceful People in the Hopi language. The Hopi spoke a language in the Shoshonean branch of the Uto-Aztecan language family.

The Hopi reservation in Arizona

The Hopi lived on the Colorado **Plateau** in northern Arizona. This land had canyons, deserts, mountain ranges, high mountain peaks, and **mesas**. Water was scarce. It came from melted snow, summer rains, and underground springs.

Today, the Hopi live on three sandstone mesas on the Colorado Plateau. The mesas rise above the desert floor. The Hopi build their homes on the mesas' flat tops. They farm on the desert floor and on terraces below the mesas.

The Hopi Homelands

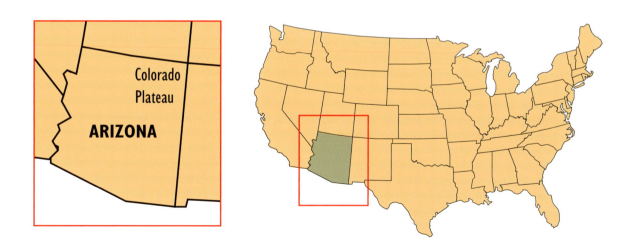

Society

The Hopi villages were called First, Second, and Third **Mesa**. First Mesa was home to the Walpi, Tewa, and Sichomovi villages. Second Mesa consisted of the Shongopavi, Mishongnovi, and Shipaulovi villages. Third Mesa included the Hotevilla, Bacavi, Moencopi, Kykotsmovi, and Oraibi villages.

In the villages, Hopi society was bound by kinship ties known as **clans**. There were many Hopi clans. Sun, Coyote, Snake, Parrot, Sand, Eagle, Rabbit, Bear, Badger, Kachina, Maasaw, Butterfly, Reed, Bow, Water, and Rain Cloud were some of the Hopi clans.

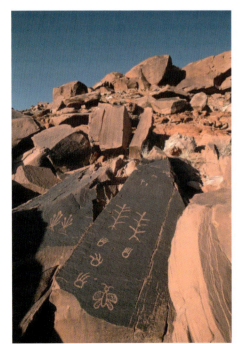

Ancient Hopi carvings of clan symbols

Each **clan** had special ceremonial duties. They performed ceremonies to give thanks. The ceremonies kept harmony between the Hopi and the natural world.

The Hopi held ceremonies in public **plazas**. Criers told other villages when ceremonies would take place. The Hopi held some ceremonies privately. They performed private ceremonies in underground chambers called **kivas**.

Each Hopi village had spiritual and political leaders. The leaders were a high priest, a priest, clan chiefs, and war chiefs. Women were spiritual leaders, too. Their duties were to keep the peace, protect the people, and continue the traditional teachings.

Food

Hopi villagers gathered, hunted, and farmed. They gathered wild tea, wild spinach, acorns, and pinyon nuts.

Hopi men hunted in the mountains and deserts. They used bows and arrows to hunt deer, bighorn sheep, pronghorn, bear, rabbit, wild turkey, quail, duck, and dove. They also used hand-woven snares to trap small animals and birds.

The Hopi practiced **dry farming**. The men cleared space for fields at the foot of the **mesas**. They used a greasewood planting stick to make holes in the soil. Then they placed the seeds in the hole. As the corn grew, they weeded the fields with wooden hoes. They watered early crops with melted snow. Later, rain came and watered the corn crops.

Blue, red, and white-kerneled corn

Over the centuries, the Hopi developed corn that grew with little water. The Hopi grew many types of corn. They grew blue corn, red corn, yellow corn, and white-kerneled sweet corn.

The women planted gardens in terraces that lined the **mesas**. Until the rains came, they watered these terrace gardens with buckets of water from natural springs.

The Hopi also planted beans, squash, and melons. Later, the Europeans brought peaches, pumpkins, apricots, and grapes. The Hopi also raised sheep and cattle.

Hopi farmers working the land

9

Homes

Hopi women built their families' houses. They built homes made from stones such as flagstone and sandstone. They took the stones from ancient ruins, or cut them from nearby **quarries**. Women set the stones with adobe mortar, and covered them with a thick layer of mud and clay.

The women covered the roofs and floors with tamarack brush and rabbit grass. Then they covered the roofs with a layer of clay two and a half feet (1 m) thick. They also covered the walls with a thick layer of clay. The clay kept the houses cool in summer and warm in winter.

Hopi families lived in the upper stories of the house. They used the bottom story for storage. They hung dried wild teas and tobacco from the

Hopi home construction

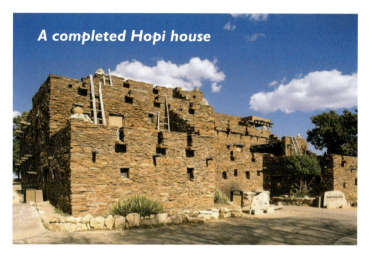
A completed Hopi house

roof beams. They slept and prepared corn in the top story.

The women shared an oven built on the outside of the home. They baked breads in the oven. The homes also connected to the **plaza** and the **kiva**, where ceremonies took place. Women built the houses close together and on top of each other. The Hopi used ladders to move from story to story in these multilevel homes. They made the ladders from juniper and pine wood. They tied the rungs to the ladder with rope woven from plant fibers.

Inside a Hopi house

Clothing

Hopi men made clothing from animal skins and woven cloth. They wove cloth from plant and animal fibers. Later, Spanish explorers brought sheep to the region. The Hopi then wove cloth from sheep's wool.

Women and girls traditionally wore a rectangular-shaped dress called a *mantra*. The dress covered the right shoulder, while the left shoulder remained bare. They wore a wide woven **sash** around the waist. On their feet, the women wore moccasins with leather wraps. The wraps wound around the ankle up to the mid-calf.

A Hopi family in traditional clothing

An unmarried Hopi woman

Men and boys traditionally wore woven shirts, leggings, and a **kilt** or **breechcloth**. Men also wrapped **sashes** around their waists. Sometimes they wore a sash across their chest, too. Men wore ankle-high moccasins with light-colored soles.

In the summer, the Hopi wore sandals woven from yucca plant leaves. In the winter, they wore rabbit-fur moccasins. They also wore woven blankets and fur robes to keep warm.

The Hopi decorated their clothing with colors and symbols that represented nature and their **culture**. They also wore shell and turquoise jewelry.

A Hopi man

Crafts

The Hopi created many kinds of arts and crafts. They carved kachina dolls and wove baskets. They also made bows and arrows, **rabbit sticks**, gourd rattles, and jewelry.

The Hopi carved kachina dolls from cottonwood tree roots. Kachina dolls represented the supernatural beings in Hopi **culture**. There were more than a hundred different kachinas. Crow Mother, Longhair, and White Corn Maiden are a few.

The Hopi outfitted each kachina doll with the type of clothing, masks, headdresses, and other items used by the kachina during ceremonial

A Hopi craftsman carves a kachina

dances. A Hopi carver needed to be very knowledgeable about his **culture** to create an **accurate** doll.

Hopi women wove beautiful baskets. They used yucca to make sifter and coil baskets. They also used wicker and rabbit brush to make plaques.

A basket plaque

Kachinas

Family

A Hopi family included the people of the entire **clan**. Hopi clans were matrilineal. This means that children belonged to their mother's clan. The women of a clan owned its gardens, homes, and possessions. They also tended to the children and prepared meals.

Though children belonged to their mother's clan, they received their names from their father's clan. This happened during a naming ceremony. This was done so that the children had an extended family to protect and teach them throughout life.

People in each clan worked together to raise and protect their children. Men prepared the fields for crops and planted the corn seeds. Women planted and harvested crops from the terrace gardens. Both men and women weeded and harvested the gardens.

Hopi were not allowed to marry members of their own clan. Once a woman agreed to marry, men from the groom's clan wove her wedding clothes. They made two sets of clothing. They rolled the second set in a reed bundle and gave it to the bride. This was called a wedding suitcase. The woman wore these clothes at her death.

Each Hopi **clan** had a special religious and political duty. Families were responsible for keeping the Hopi traditional teachings alive. These teachings included dances and songs. They required people to be humble, work in cooperation, and respect and protect Mother Earth.

A Hopi mother and her baby

Children

Hopi children learned from their parents, grandparents, aunts and uncles, **clan** elders, and religious leaders. They learned Hopi dances, songs, and **culture** as a part of their daily lives.

A game of field hockey

Women taught the girls how to cook, grind corn, and care for babies. The girls played with kachina dolls. The dolls taught the girls about the different kachinas and the Hopi culture.

Men taught the boys traditional Hopi ways. The boys learned how to make and use

rabbit sticks and bows and arrows. They painted their bows with the traditional white, blue, yellow, and purple stripes.

Boys and girls played games to develop their minds and bodies. One popular game was darts. They made the

A Hopi mother styles her daughter's hair

darts from corn cobs, and tied feathers on the end. The children threw the darts at a target.

Children also played a type of field hockey. They used a hickory stick, and a ball made from corn husks. They built goals by arranging stones in a semi-circle. The children buried the ball in the center of the field. The game began once the ball was dug out. The object of the game was to get the ball into the other team's goal.

Myths

The Hopi emergence story tells how the Hopi came to this world. They traveled through three worlds to get to the Fourth World. Animals and insects helped the Hopi survive.

The First World was colored white. There, Dawa and Spider Woman created human beings. The humans were told to pray to the gods, take care of the land, and use only what they needed. When the humans forgot to follow these instructions, Dawa destroyed the First World.

Blue Ants helped the humans live in the Second World. The Ants taught the people how to build homes from rock and clay. But soon the people stopped praying to the gods and caring for the land. Food became scarce. The Ants gave the people their food and tightened their belts. That is why ants have such tiny waists. But since the humans had forgotten to pray and care for the land, Dawa destroyed the Second World.

In the Third World, the people forgot to pray and do the dances. So Dawa dried up all the water and vegetation.

Everything turned yellow. Dawa told the men to go down into the **kivas** to find a new place to live. The men prayed and were visited by different birds and animals that would later become the **clans**.

Hopi Point in the Grand Canyon

The men saw an opening above them but they could not reach it. Birds tried to reach the opening, but they could not. Chipmunk, who had many seeds, planted a reed. The reed grew tall enough to reach the opening. The Hopi climbed up the reed and entered the Fourth World, which is represented by the color purple.

Today, the Hopi believe they are living in the Fourth World. They are caretakers, and not owners, of the land. They must continue to pray and dance as Dawa instructed. The opening into the Fourth World is called the *sipapu*. It is located in the Grand Canyon.

War

The Hopi were a peaceful people. They did not like war. Their spiritual beliefs taught them to live in harmony with other people and nature.

The Hopi's remote location on the **mesas** helped keep them safe from **intruders**. From the top of the mesas, the Hopi could see a long distance. They could easily see approaching enemies.

From time to time, the Hopi had to protect themselves from hostile tribes. Often the Hopi had to defend themselves against Apache and Navajo **raids**. These tribes robbed Hopi villages. They captured women and children, and sold them into slavery.

In 1680, the Hopi joined Pueblo tribes to fight the Spaniards. The Spaniards wanted to control the Hopi and convert them to Christianity. The Hopi fought to protect their land and **culture**. Many people died. This war is known today as the Pueblo Revolt.

Hopi weapons

Contact with Europeans

The Spaniards were the first Europeans to make contact with the Hopi. In the 1540s, Spanish explorer Francisco Vásquez de Coronado came to the southwest looking for cities that were full of gold.

Coronado heard about the Hopi villages. He sent a small expedition led by Pedro de Tovar to find them. Tovar returned to Coronado with the disappointing news that the Hopi villages were not full of gold.

In the 1600s, Spanish **missionaries** tried to convert the Hopi to Christianity. But the Hopi had strong religious beliefs and practices. So they would not convert to the new religion.

The United States acquired the Hopi homelands from the Spaniards. **Raids** into their lands by the Navajo continued. In 1850, a group of Hopi leaders asked the U.S. government for help. The next year, the U.S. built Fort Defiance. The fort protected white settlers, and protected the Hopi from Navajo raids.

During the Civil War, the U.S. abandoned Fort Defiance. The Navajo began to **raid** the Hopi villages again. The raids threatened the Hopi's survival. So in 1864, the Hopi again sought help from the U.S. government.

But the U.S. government did not understand what the Hopi wanted. They were treated rudely and imprisoned. Many Hopi died from hunger and diseases the soldiers brought to their land.

Francisco Vásquez de Coronado explores the southwest.

Yokiuma

Yokiuma was keeper of the **sacred** stone tablet. His duty was to protect and maintain the sacred teachings of the Hopi people. He and his followers worked hard to protect the Hopi way of life.

Yokiuma and his followers fought against American interference in the Hopi **culture**. So the U.S. government called Yokiuma and his followers Hostiles. Hopi who went along with the government's policies and programs were called Friendlies.

Yokiuma and his followers did not want to send Hopi children away to American boarding schools. Children at the schools were not allowed to visit home. Yokiuma feared the children would forget the Hopi language and culture. This endangered the Hopi way of life. The U.S. government jailed many Hopi parents when they refused to send their children to the schools.

The Friendlies and the Hostiles argued in the Hopi villages. The tension between Yokiuma and the Friendlies in the Oraibi village led to the creation of a new village. In 1906, Yokiuma and his followers established a village called Hotevilla.

Hopi **culture** has survived due to leaders like Yokiuma. Although Yokiuma has died, his wish to protect the Hopi way of life continues in Hotevilla. The Hopi believe that their original prayers, songs, and dances need to be maintained not only for the Hopi, but for the survival of the world.

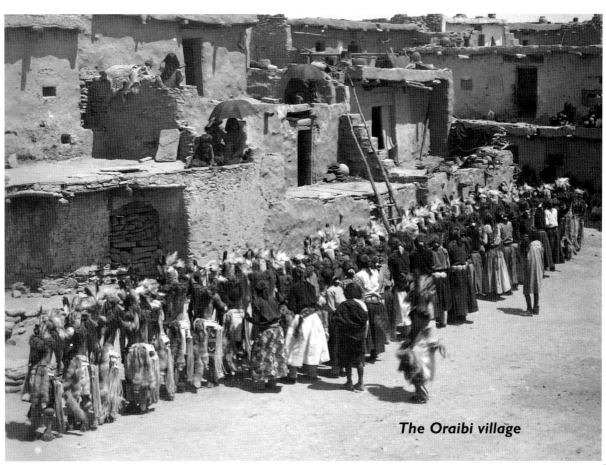

The Oraibi village

The Hopi Today

In 1882, U.S. President Chester A. Arthur created the Hopi **Reservation**. It covers 2,439 square miles (6,317 sq km). Today, 12,500 members of the Hopi tribe live there.

In 1936, the Hopi Tribal Council was established. This form of government has a **constitution** like the U. S. Constitution, and it is recognized by the U. S. government.

Today, Hopi children do not have to be sent away to boarding schools to get an education. Schools have been built on the **mesas**. Since the children are not sent away to school, they can participate in community and ceremonial activities.

During ceremonies, most Hopi villages are closed to the public. But the public is invited to the mesas during most social dances. To preserve their **culture**, the Hopi do not allow photographs to be taken of their villages or ceremonies.

Hopi baskets and pottery are beautifully colored with natural dyes made from charcoal, sand, flower petals, and other plants. They contain colors and symbols that represent Hopi culture.

Kachina dolls are carved with a sharp knife. Then they are painted with colors made from natural materials. Colors like blue, green, and red were made from ground stones. Black was made from ashes, and white was made from clay. They used yucca leaf paint brushes.

Preserving their **culture** is very important to the Hopi. The Hopi language is an important part of their traditional ceremonies. To help preserve the language, the Hopi have written a dictionary with over 30,000 words. Children also learn their language in school.

Many Hopi go into the **urban** areas to find work. They return to the **mesas** for ceremonies. Some Hopi parents have created dance groups. These dance groups teach the urban Hopi children the traditional dances, songs, and other Hopi cultural ways. This way, the modern Hopi people can participate in and maintain their traditional way of life.

Hopi author Helen Sequaptawa

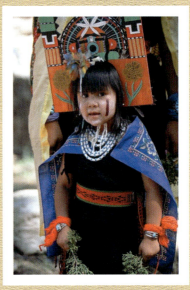

This girl is dressed to participate in the Hopi Butterfly Dance.

Glossary

accurate - free of errors.

breechcloth - a piece of hide or cloth, usually worn by men, that was wrapped between the legs and tied with a belt around the waist.

clan - a group of families in a community that have common ancestors.

constitution - the laws that govern a country.

culture - the customs, arts, and tools of a nation or people at a certain time.

dry farming - farming on nonirrigated land by planting drought-resistant crops and turning under soil wet with dew or rain.

intruder - a person who comes in without invitation or welcome.

kilt - a skirt worn by men that reaches to the knees.

kiva - a ceremonial structure that is usually round and partly underground.

mesa - a flat-topped hill or mountain with steep sides.

missionary - a person who spreads a church's religion.

plateau - a raised area of flat land.

plaza - a public square or open space in a community.

quarry - a place where stone is cut from the earth for use in building.

rabbit stick - a weapon thrown at a running rabbit's legs that snares the legs and trips the rabbit, keeping it from running away so the hunter can catch it.

raid - a sudden attack.

reservation - a piece of land set aside by the government for Native Americans to live on.

sacred - spiritual or religious.

sash - a wide piece of cloth used like a belt.

urban - having to do with a city.

Web Sites

Official Site of the Hopi Tribe: http://www.hopi.nsn.us/

Official Hopi Cultural Preservation Office Home Page:
http://www.nau.edu/~hcpo-p/index.html#table

These sites are subject to change. Go to your favorite search engine and type in Hopi for more sites.

Index

A
Apache 22
art 14
Arthur, Chester A. 28

B
Bacavi 6
basket weaving 15

C
ceremonies 7, 11, 14, 16, 28
children 12, 13, 16, 18, 19, 22,
    26, 28, 30
Civil War 25
clans 6, 7, 16, 17, 18, 21
cloth weaving 12
clothing 12, 13, 17
Coronado, Francisco
    Vásquez de 24
crafts 14, 15
crops 8, 9, 16
culture 13, 14, 15, 18, 22, 26,
    27, 28, 30

E
emergence story 20, 21
Europeans 22, 24

F
family 6, 10, 11, 16, 17, 18
farming 5, 8, 9, 16
First Mesa 6
food 8, 11, 18, 20
Fort Defiance 24, 25

G
games 19

H
home construction 10, 11
homelands 5, 6, 22, 24
homes 5, 10, 11
Hopi Tribal Council 28
Hotevilla 6, 26, 27
hunting 8

K
kachina dolls 14, 15, 18
kiva 7, 11, 21
Kykotsmovi 6

L
language 4, 26, 30
leaders 7, 18

M
marriage 16, 17
mesas 5, 6, 8, 9, 22, 28, 30
Mishongnovi 6
Moencopi 6

N
Navajo 22, 24, 25

O
Oraibi 6, 26

P
Pueblo 22
Pueblo Revolt 22

R
religion 17, 22, 24
reservations 28

S
Second Mesa 6
Shipaulovi 6
Shongopavi 6
Sichomovi 6
social organization 6, 7, 16, 17

T
Tewa 6
Third Mesa 6
Tovar, Pedro de 24
traditional teachings 7, 17, 18,
    19, 26, 27

U
United States government 24,
    25, 26, 28

W
Walpi 6
war 22, 24, 25

Y
Yokiuma 26, 27